Enchanted with your beauty
I gaze at you –
dark eyes,
black hair,
all lit up with laughter.

Waswanipi

Songs of a Scattered People
by Hugo Muller

The Anglican Book Centre
Toronto, Canada

Copyright © 1976
The Anglican Book Centre
600 Jarvis Street
Toronto, Ontario
Canada M4Y 2J6
ISBN 0-919030-15-7

CONTENTS

PREFACE

It is really within the present generation, that twentieth century society has swept in among the inland Cree people of north western Quebec, who up to that time had experienced only sporadic and limited contact with western society. The Church had been there for many generations, and so had the Hudson's Bay Company, but apart from them and some government employees, that was the extent of the contact. Then, within the last two decades, mines were discovered, roads constructed, and towns built — Chapais, Chibougamau, Quevillon, Joutel, Matagami — all on the traditional hunting grounds. Now the James Bay hydro project is changing everything.

Apart from all the other important questions, there looms the most disturbing one: why a civilization which has produced a Leonardo da Vinci, a Shakespeare and a Beethoven, seems to destroy any other culture it comes into contact with. For that, I have not found the answer. I have just lived through the tragedies, and if there appears a great emphasis on death and liquor, then that is because they are such everyday parts of life in these places.

These songs and stories tell what happens when twentieth century progress hits the traditional hunting life of a people known for their passive and gentle ways, their politeness and reticence, which we often find hard to understand. Names have been changed, but all events relate to actual happenings.

I want to express my thanks to those who have helped with suggestions, and who have supplied photographs. The pictures in many instances are not professional but do give a view of some of the people and places in the text. The children and adults in these photographs have no connection in any way with the events related.

This is, admittedly, only one side of a story with many facets, but a side too often forgotten. If it strikes you as sad, and even bitter, I cannot apologize for that. Studdert-Kennedy said it well in one of his sermons: "I cannot stand the civilized method of being savage." For this is what is happening in these places. We are witnessing one of the greatest cultural tragedies in Canadian history — and no doubt the sins of the fathers will be visited upon the children.

To the Cree people and their survival this work is dedicated, with my deep gratitude for the many ways in which they have enriched my life, and with my prayer that the amazing resilience of the Indian way of life may yet triumph over the worst we are doing to it.

Skyhook

It was a quick fire
from that overheated cord
strung from shack to shack,
with which they shared
a bit of electricity
among too many.
That's the way it is
in those shacktowns –
you improvise
and do what you can.

Those tar-paper shacks
are firetraps.
Sophie got out
with three-year old Andrew,
but Sarah died
in the flames
though they tried hard,
and Billy cut his wrists
trying to rip down the wall
with his hands,
and Joe's hair was singed
and there were burns
all over his face.

The police said
to ship the body out –
a hundred and twenty miles
to the big hospital
for an autopsy –
whatever that would do.

But at least that way
we got a casket
for the mutilated body,
and it saved us
that always
heart-breaking experience
of picking up
from the hospital
a body in a cardboard box
or even an old blanket,
and putting the dead child
ourselves
into the home-made
plywood coffin,
with the parents
each solemnly
fastening a screw
on the lid.

So I picked up
the little casket
which had to stay closed,
and drove the long way back
with the sad load,
to bury Sarah
who had lived
all of one year.

It was a very bleak day
in November,
already hard
to dig a grave
in the freezing earth.

After the church service
we gathered
at the graveside
for the few final prayers
the committal
and the filling in
of the grave.
We were close together –
a sad little huddle –
for it was a time
of drawing near.

As I began the prayers
just beyond,
a huge helicopter
dragonfly with wings clipped
(they call it a Skyhook) –
one,
two thousand dollars
an hour? –
lifted off
swinging drums of fuel
underneath the skeleton frame,
all for La Baie James –
proud
overpowering symbol
of Hydro,
of millions of dollars.

The monster
drowned out our prayers,
the sound
shaking the air around us,
slashing viciously
into our bodies.

And we waited
and Sophie stood
very still,
noble in her sorrow
as few I have ever seen.
But something inside me
cried out so loud
I thought it would be heard
even above the noise,
that fearsome noise
that shattered
more than silence.

Of course
the very large project
could not wait
till we had buried
the very small child.
The very expensive helicopter
took priority
over the very cheap life.

The skyhook,
almost as if
momentarily embarrassed
of invading this sad moment,
roared awkwardly away
ungainly swaying
with the heavy load,
rattled off
over the treetops
which cringed
and shivered
under its hideous shadow.
And all the while
it muttered incomprehensibly
of progress
and development
and construction deadlines.

Then
we resumed
our prayers –
and buried
Sarah.

James Bay Is Go

That twentieth century symphony
named Progress
will be played again –
Biggest performance ever!
Never before on this scale!

The angry roar of the bulldozers
is the deafening leitmotif.

The winds and brass –
those warning sirens
blasting intermittently,
sounding their apocalyptic wails –
for the Last Days have come
for the land.

And then the drums –
irregular, maladjusted
in the muffled roars of exploding rock
as the land groans in agony.

The string section –
the whining of the power saws
screeching in incredible falsetto.

And even a chorus –
the shouting and cursing
of construction crews
loud, obscene, offensive,
and the little Indian kids
picking up the filthy words
like garbage from the cookeries –
and it soils them
the same way.

Everything loud, overpowering
drowning out the anguished moans
of a violated land.
And soon the dams will rise
dark and threatening,
killing the rivers
which will cease to play
their white and silver games
in the rapids and the falls.

Dark, inexorable waters
will flood
the trapping grounds
the campsites
the place where Linda was born
where old Sally was buried
where Isaac shot his first caribou
where people lived and loved
and sang hymns and prayed
and were happy on their land.

The symphony continues incessantly
without beat, without rhythm –
not music, only poisoned noise
not melody, but a cacophony
of chaotic, polluted sound –
so people may plug in
their air conditioners and computers
their electric guitars and neon lights
and light up their store windows
glittering with idols.

And no silence will ever fall again
for the wind will whistle on, evermore
through the high tension wires
and aluminum towers,
its song sad
and its message
empty.

Homecoming

The June sun
rises early
full of promise,
laughing itself
through the morning fog
into dawn.
Today the kids come home
from residential school.

Some parents
have been drinking.
It's hard to face your children
who have grown into strangers –
hard for them, also.
No one ever knows
what to say
what to do
where to look
those first few moments.

That awkward joyfulness
is still to come.
Now, there is only dark water
covered with white
where the green canoes
splash their way,
each at his own speed,
to the dock where the road ends –
where the other world begins.

From the other side –
out of the white man's world
through endless rows
of jackpine and spruce
(their colour dull
because of the young green
of poplar and willow and birch) –
comes the yellow schoolbus
packed with children
excited, nervous,
most sitting quietly.
But their looks betray
what is in their hearts.

At the water's edge
the two worlds meet,
the yellow schoolbus
and the green canoe,
the children streaming
from one world
into the other –
from the neatly made beds
in well kept dormitories
to sleeping bags on spruce bows
or rough wooden floors,
from carefully controlled hours
and contrived activities
to the freedom of home,
from one world
into another.
For the road ends at the dock
where the waters begin,
and there is no connection.

Standing back,
I watched them
pouring out
of the yellow schoolbus –
a happy flood of kids.
Then once more
they became individuals
as each stepped carefully
into a different green canoe.

I had to return that day
and got a ride on the schoolbus.
It was hollow and forsaken,
empty as the world
we were entering once more,
but their canoes
and their shacks were full –
and also their hearts.

Baptism and Burial

There was joy in the tent
when that winter I went
in cold such as no one could fancy,
where swaddled she lay
born the previous day –
so I baptized Elizabeth Nancy.

But life in the wild
is severe for a child,
with rigours as no one could fancy.
Soon we scraped down to moss
and placed a small cross
with the name of Elizabeth Nancy.

But the Cree people, wise
know that in the big skies
in happiness no one can fancy,
she now plays with Johnny
and Philomene and Lonnie,
our lovely Elizabeth Nancy.

The Vision

Enchanted with your beauty
I gaze at you –
dark eyes
black hair
all lit up with laughter
as you play
and run about the camp –
lovely butterfly dancing
and just as fragile.

And a deep, dark dread
sweeps over me.

For already
you are condemned –
sleeping on the floor
of a tar-paper shack,
while my children rest
in their soft
cozy beds.
And when at night
I tuck them in
I think of you,
and fear stabs viciously
again,
for you are Cree
and the world
has little
for you.

Your beauty –
that sad, sweet glory
of the Cree –
will soon attract
the worst of men.
And where will I find you
ten, twelve years
from now?

Will I sit with you
in hospital
after your first
or second
or third baby? –
innocent
unbelievably beautiful children,
born out of senseless
drunken binges,
'father unknown'
as we call these men
on our official forms.
(Perhaps just as well,
for what other name
can we give
to those who ravish
and destroy
and maim?)

Or will I pick you up
from jail? –
your eyes still dull
with last night's alcohol,
your hair dishevelled
and your body bruised –
to take you home
to nothing.

I fear, my God.
I am afraid
of all that is to come –
afraid for you
for others,
a hopeless
overwhelming fear
that all beauty
will be destroyed,
all innocence
raped and soiled.

And a helpless anger
rises in my heart
for you
and your people,
victims of a culture
which is mine,
of which I am a part,
for which I also
must bear the guilt –
the burden
of all who destroy.

And I can only pray,
Lord, have mercy
on these
thy people,
Lord have mercy
on this
thy child.

Lord have mercy
on me.

Erlking

She walked by the shore
in sunset's glow
to look for the plane
ordered two days ago.
She held Marcel
in her young loving arms,
and rocked him gently
keeping him warm.

'O mama!
The windigos there I see.
Their cold, clammy fingers
reach for me!'
'Hush, baby, hush child,
everything is all right –
it is only the fog
that comes in the night.'

'O mama!
The roar of a giant nearby.
A monster is coming,
there – in the sky!'
'Be quiet, Marcel.
There's no need to fear –
it's only the airplane
coming near.'

The plane picked them up
and left right away –
the pilot explained
the long delay.
'We got the message
on Friday night,
but no one was there
to vouch for flight.'

The plane droned on
as darkness fell,
Marcel crying wild
in fevered spell.
His mother still soothed him
though growing afraid.
The pilot cursed softly –
and then he prayed.

The sky was alight
with many a star –
it was late when I rushed them
into the car.
As we raced to the hospital
nothing was said.
We both knew Marcel
already was dead.

The Hitch-Hiker

He walked along the road –
forty miles to get that far
forty miles on snowshoes
through the bush
in thirty below
and only two brief stops –
a quickly made fire
some tea
and a piece of banik.

He tried to get a ride
but few cars passed.
It was close to four
in the afternoon
(and thirty below) –
a lonely stretch of road
on Saturday evening.

Some did pass by
but in a hurry.
They thought,
'Look at that Indian
trying to get to the hotel.
Wants his beer tonight
I bet you.

Let's not smell up our car
with a dirty Indian' –
torn windbreaker
frayed cap
and trousers
from the missionary bale,
snowshoes over the shoulder
swaying from the axe handle,
mocassins treading wearily
on the packed road.
(Perhaps they were afraid
of the axe.)

The taxi driver stopped –
he knew Jean Baptiste.
He knew them all.
Even if Jean Baptiste was broke
the driver wouldn't leave him
out in the cold.

He had a heart
that taxi driver.
The Indians all liked him,
always asked him
to drive for them.
They called him Machi-manitoo
'devil'
because he was so ugly.
But they trusted him.
He was good
and honest,
taking care of things –
collecting mail,
picking up cheques
for those in the bush,
sending money orders
to the kids
in residential school.

Jean Baptiste
did not want beer
that night.
He wanted a plane.
His kid
he was very sick,
and Jean Baptiste
had snowshoed forty miles
to get help.
The driver told the manager
at the air base.
But winters are long
and very dark in the north,
and it was too late
to fly that night,
and too many cars
had passed by
when there still was time.

The next day it snowed
and Jean Baptiste waited,
But when at last
they flew in
his kid was dead.

In the solitude
of his church
the priest asked God
for strength –
help
for yet another burial.
It was the third child
in three weeks.

After they buried the baby
there was more waiting
to get back to the bush,
and Jean Baptiste
finally went
to the hotel.
As he came staggering out
those who had passed him
on the road happened by.
'Look,' they said.
'There's that Indian.
Got his beer all right,
didn't he?'

A little later
the police picked him up,
and Jean Baptiste went to jail.
He had no more money –
and he had no more kids.

Don't knock a man down and then ask why
he lies in the dirt. Don't strip a man of his
clothing and then ask why he is naked. Don't
filch a man of his authority, his right to rule
his home, his dignity as a man, and then ask
him why his culture is substandard. (From a
speech by Chief Dan George, at Williams
Lake, B.C. in the UNITED CHURCH NEWSLETTER,
November 1966)

Matagami

Move over Indian.
You are primitive
backward
and uncivilized.
You have committed
the unpardonable sin –
you have left your land
as it was
in all its untaimed beauty –
you have not developed it.

You had your chance.
What did you people
ever contribute
to this country?
What did you make of it, huh?
Now we will take over,
for we are civilized
and technologically sophisticated,
and progress and development
can't be stopped.
Imagine –
you do not even have words
for these concepts!

We are coming!
And we shall strangle the rivers
and choke the creeks.
We shall slash the trees
and burn the slash
and drown the land.
We shall kill the game
and rip the rocks apart
with dynamite,
and carve our initials
all over the land –
in roads
and railways
and hydro right-of-ways.

Burn, baby, burn.
Flood, baby, flood.
For we are civilized
and you are backward.
We shall build
the proud new towns
that tell of our mastery
over nature –
over you.

But it was the Lord
who planted a garden.
And it was Cain –
his brother's murderer –
who built the city,
wasn't it?

The cities we want to build –
with ghettos
and inner city problems
and traffic congestion
and endless, wandering suburbs
laid out in neat monotony,
where men play golf
on weekends
and wives are always bored –
cities with drug addicts
and crime
and violence
and poverty
screaming back
at police sirens
in hideous dissonance,
where one cannot walk
alone
at night.

For we
are civilized.

The White Man

Along the road
leading north to Chapais
there's an old bush camp
where Cree Indians stay.
And among the children
the first you will see
is a boy with blue eyes
who speaks only Cree.

Mary was young
and Mary was pretty –
she went with a white man
away to the city.
But as it happens
with most of them there
she was back – with a kid –
in just over a year.

The boy had blue eyes
and light blond hair.
His skin was white
and his looks were fair,
and so he remained
as he grew day by day –
they nicknamed him White Man
for such is their way.

It was around New Year
that tragedy fell,
for Mary went down
to the nearest hotel.
She sat and she drank
and she acted queer,
but no one would tell her
she'd had enough beer.

Always she listened
and when from afar
she heard the sound
of an oncoming car,
she'd rush out and look
to see who was there,
then slowly walk back
and order more beer.

She ran really fast
when she rushed for the truck.
It was just a light pick-up
but heavy it struck.
She never did see
who it was inside –
for she hit the snowbank
and there she died.

The driver was shaken.
He tried to explain –
he'd slammed on the brakes
and signaled in vain.
The police were French,
like the witnesses three.
What chance do you have?
You've had beer and you're Cree.

So Mary was buried
and her parents took care
of the little white man
with the light blond hair.
And still to this day
in their camp you will see
a fair, blue-eyed boy
who speaks only Cree.

New Year's Message

But just a minute
you Indians and Inuit.
When we say
there is room for all
in this country
to pursue their dreams,
that means Anglophones
Francophones
New Canadians
but not necessarily
Native Canadians.

For you must integrate
assimilate.
You must share
in our dreams
of progress,
which for you
may be a nightmare,
effectively eliminating you
and your dreams.

You are not allowed
to retain your culture
in our bicultural society
(which we call multicultural
when we need the ethnic vote),
for you do not matter.

Nobody speaks your language.
You have no money.
No one needs your vote.
You have only land
and we take
what we want.
Nobody protests –
that would be
politically inexpedient.
And we can always say,
'You can't stop progress.'

Send your children
to our schools
to learn our language,
our ways –
so we can civilize
the little savages.
Our way may be foreign
but our way is best –
our way of competition
of ambition
greed
envy
and pride.

Send your kids
to the white men's towns
where they learn to steal
to cheat
to lie –
where they can become
drug addicts –
for our way is best.

When we talk
of different life-styles
we do not mean your style.
We mean legalizing homo-sexuality
and abortion on demand,
and putting sex offenders
on parole.
Your life style
we do not want,
for it condemns our own.

You can laugh
when you have nothing,
and you can love
without books to say how,
and your older people
do not steal
or damage the environment,
and in your life-style
there are no unwanted children,
and the old aren't put away
in institutions,
and the young respect the old.

So forget about your dreams.
They are doomed
to be shattered
under the bulldozer tracks,
fated to turn into a nightmare
of cultural genocide,
because you can't stop progress.

You
move over.
Yours is the only place
where there is still peace,
and we must destroy it –
this is our mission –
for there is no peace
for the wicked.
We cannot have it.
Why should you?

We have lost our innocence.
You must lose yours
and dream our dreams –
sugared with tranquillizers
soothed with sleeping pills –
while your land lies
drowned and raped,
and the cries of little ones
are lost
in the roar of progress
that can't be stopped.

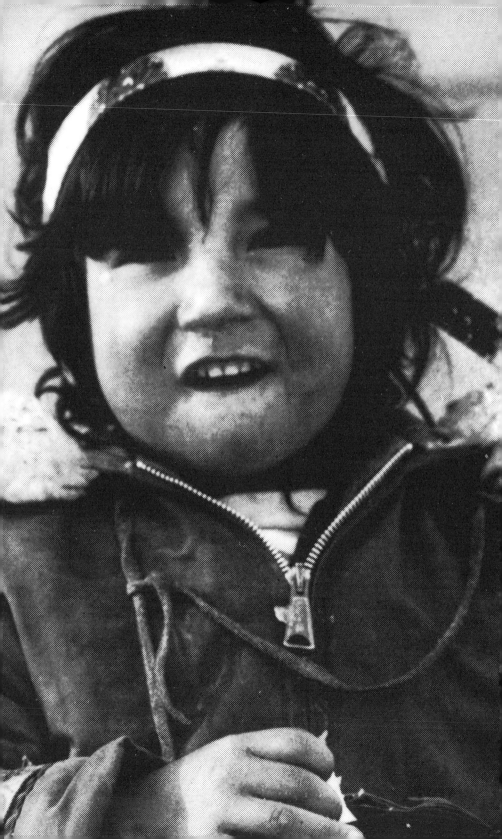

Chicki

She was a lovely
little girl,
but she had this limp
that made her hobble
grotesquely.

I talked with the doctor.
'Yes, one of those hip-deformations.
It happens with these Indians
the way they carry their babies.
It should be operated, soon
before she is six years –
the sooner the better.'
I learned about it
as much as I could,
then went to sit down
in the little shack
to explain it –
their way.

They agreed,
perhaps because
they trusted me,
and that summer
little Chicki was packed off
to the hospital far away.
She was there a long time –
very long indeed.

I remember
when she came back.
The taxi driver told me
she was at the bus stop.
(The nurses
never seemed to know
where these people
were living.)
I picked her up happily
to bring her home.

She knew her parents.
Recognition –
that shy happiness –
was in her face.
But she could not talk
to them.
She did not understand
the Cree.
She only spoke French now.
The language
long unheard
was forgotten.

And she limped
even worse
than before.
Her parents saw it.
I knew already
and that too was a shock,
though it was only temporary
and it did disappear,
and Chicki walked straight
after some time.

I remember
the first day she ran
at the pow-wow.
She came last
and we gave her
first prize.

Yet I wondered
about my meddling.
It was the first time
I had to interpret
between a mother
and her child.

Nannish

The April sun
is warm already,
staining the snow
striking the ice
with merciless challenge
to its long mastery.

In the little village
sheltered in the hollow
of the age-old hills,
Nannish ventures out
searching for the rickety chair,
her stick in those amazing hands
gnarled and worn
yet so strangely beautiful.

Her eyes are misted over
with the uncertainties
of the twentieth century.
She doesn't see much anymore.
Her steps are slow and uncertain.
Her hands tremble a little,
and her face
furrowed in a hundred folds –
she was a pretty girl
last century.

How old she is
no one knows for certain.
They say almost ninety.
Some say more
far more,
but no one can remember
that far back –
not even Nannish.

She sits
outside the little shack
in the timelessness
of her world,
the eternal April sun
loving her face
into yet another spring.
Years have nothing to say
and Nannish says nothing.
Even her eyes
have this mist over them,
veiling their depths.

What is there to say
of all the winters
in the hunt camp
of all the summers
by the lake
of all the trips
to the trading post
of all the children
she has cared for
of all the burdens carried
of all the sorrows borne.

It's all there
within her
as she sits
motionless as time,
only her eyes blinking.
It is her –
strange, sweet
mellowed, strong
unfathomable.

I wonder,
does she sit there again
this April,
or will she too have gone
taking more than herself? –
the memories unspoken
of the life unknown
of her people
unwanted.
The April sun
will miss her –
and so will I.

Octopus

The fat
throbbing
megalopolitan octopus
stretches out,
unnumbered tentacles
groping into the north,
seeking more
always more
to satisfy
insatiable greed.

And thus the roads
reach winding
into the north,
searching for the food
that will not satisfy.

First the ugly slashes.
Then the gravel –
dust settling on the trees,
the land clothing itself
in sackcloth and ashes.
Then finally –
provided there are
the right political connections –
the black asphalt
running forlornly,
but always ending
where the tentacles have found
new energy
new blood
to draw from the land.

Highways are meant to be
connections, links
that draw together
that mutually enrich.
Here they are funnels
to draw out
empty the land
to fill the monster far away.

Lumber trucks are always first,
loaded beyond prudence
staggering under the wood –
living trees to make
dead paper.

Traffic multiplies
on the face of the earth,
a never ceasing procession
sweeping in
to take out –
cars, stationwagons
filled with fish,
the daily bread
of the people.
The lakes are emptying
but who cares.
We paid the province
our licence fees
and the guide his tip
and a bottle of booze.

In fall come the cars –
mooseheads on hoods,
congealed blood caked
on proud antlers,
empty eyes
staring
at empty people,
and a few steaks
to fill stomachs
that were never empty.

We just want the trophy –
the rest can rot in the bush.
We do not need to eat –
we only want to kill.

Half a winter's food
for Philip and his family,
the hide that was to be
Andrew's moccasins
Georgie's mitts
Lillian's snowshoes –
rotting in the bush.
It goes on –
caribou, deer
stiff, cold, lifeless
dismembered.
Proud geese
strung up
like a bunch of onions,
fish packed in ice.
(Even the ice
is taken away.)

Always
everything goes south,
drawn ever faster
by that insatiable suction
into the vacuum
far away.

Nothing comes back,
for even the new towns
are parasites on the land –
drawing from it
giving nothing.
We even spend our money
down below
where the cities are,
and that is
where we shall retire.

Trucks and trains with ore
rumble through days and nights.
Even below the surface
the octopus sucks empty the land.

The rivers dammed
and damned,
turbines whirring,
wires carrying invisible power
into the heaving mass far south –
so it can pulsate
with coloured lights
and advertise
its blue movies
and its yellow morals.

Nothing returns.
For we have nothing to give –
we can only take.
That's what happens
when you believe
a man's life consists
in the abundance
of his possessions.

And the octopus
is very demanding
in its hideous strength,
and we serve it dutifully.
But inspite of all we take
we are emptier
than ever.

The One Who
Came With The Geese

Chill winter wished to linger
and grimly hindered spring,
still gripped with clinging finger
and bitter winds that sting.

In spite, the geese were arriving
with wings blinding white on the skies,
their bodies with force northward driving,
and wild their exuberant cries.

The lakes made haste in waking
to break their pale embrace
that quavered, quailing, quaking –
to winsome waves gave place.

She was born in the first light of dawning
on the day when the first geese came by,
and her cries mixed with theirs on that morning
writing life on the brightening sky.

Hunters' guns boomed in wild jubilation –
in the spring camp the feast would not cease –
and they named her, in sweet inspiration,
The-one-who-came-with-the-geese.

Three years she lived and enraptured –
the eyes of the child of the Cree!
till death in jealousy captured
what in envy he would not let be.

She went home in the moon of October
when the fall flocks flew over once more,
and the hunt camp lay lonesome and sober
as her body we solemnly bore.

We came to the grave and stood praying –
a lone goose flew low in the sky –
and choked were the words we were saying,
and haunting his heart-rending cry.

Cold snow came slowly blowing,
erased the grave's sad trace
and cooled the hot tears flowing
on every anguished face.

Each spring that the geese keep bringing,
with wings blinding white on the skies,
I desire to delight in their singing –
cold sorrow replies.

Reminder

When God thought of making
the little Cree children,
He took special care
in creating their eyes,
and to tell of the mystery
of lands never trodden,
He plucked some aurora
from subarctic skies.

He left out that innocence
one finds in the carefree
and put in a darkness,
a silent, sad sigh
of hardships unwritten
and joys long forgotten –
the haunting lament
of a race doomed to die.

He put there the stillness
of snows and of waters,
the splash of the beaver
the call of the moose,
the sweep of the rivers
the sparkling of rapids,
the song of the frog
and the flight of the goose.

He created the darkness
of long, lonely winters,
the inscrutable depths
of a culture so strange.
He wrote a reminder
for all men to ponder –
it is theirs to retain
and not ours to change.

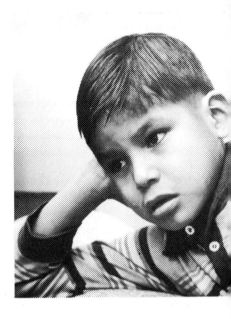

Anik

High,
high in the sky –
higher
than the eagle will fly,
beyond the reach
of Northern Lights
swings Anik,
innocent
in tiny brightness.

The latest
of satellites,
providing the latest
to entertain –
late movies
and lovin' spoonfuls
of commercials
for bright bright toothpaste
white white detergent
fast fast pain relief
liquid to take away dandruff
CBC Canadian Content
and all the rest.

Now it beams all that
from its lofty heights,
not only
to a pseudo-sophisticated south
but to a people far away,
to civilize the Indian
with ads for Molson Golden,
and the Eskimo
with documentaries
on the Two Solitudes.

Anik,
we call it –
see
even an Eskimo name,
'Brother' –
to reach a brotherly hand
across this wasteland,
these backward people
never developed.
Look what **we** can do!
See how **we** live!
Why don't **you**?

Anik, Brother –
big brother?
or a brother
like that first one
in the Bible,
the one whose offering
was not received by God,
the one who envied
his brother
and murdered him.

Anik, Brother,
now calling all brothers
in the north.
Anik, Brother,
technological marvel,
murdering brothers
with a living-colour smile.

The Road

Spring had come early.
The geese were returning,
filling the skies
with their glorious sound.
Everywhere water
was running and rustling.
Snowdrifts were sinking
in wet, spongy ground.

Slowly they walked
in the sunshine of morning –
the young girl
already a mother of three,
the mother, too old
to bear any more children,
stooped in the sorrow
that is part of the Cree.

They walked from the bush camp
along the new highway,
from the tent in the bush
to the shack near the town –
forty-two miles –
and they hoped for a car ride.
Cars there passed many,
but none would slow down.

The silence was such
one could hear the cars coming,
and when they were near
the women would turn.
But they only looked –
they would not lift a finger.
Such is their way –
which we will not learn.

Far was Matagami,
boom-town exploding –
James Bay and Hydro –
at dizzying speed,
quickly their culture
and life style eroding,
ravaging all
with a fierce, savage greed.

All the time trucks went by –
long were their trailers –
with ready made houses
and hordes of supply.
Just in the hour
the women had walked there,
a home for each one
of their people passed by.

'Sorry,' officials
will say of these matters.
'It's off-reserve land
where these people live.
Certainly housing
will soon be provided.
First get the land,'
(which the province won't give).

It's only for warehouse
and depot and Hydro,
only for men
who will build the Baie James,
not for the Natives,
'les maudits sauvages.'
None would consider
their outdated claims.

Onward they rolled –
the trucks and their trailers –
passing the women,
passing them by.
Yet these two smiled
in the spring and the sunshine.
I noticed them smiling –
I wondered why.

Suzanne

Here is beauty.
You have it –
unknowingly.

Not the sultry
evocative appeal
to the senses,
like the cover-girl
on the slick
fashion magazine,
nor the self-assured poise
of the wealthy,
who wear it
along with the mink coat
(as the inherent right
of the affluent),
not even the innocent
laughing beauty
of the child –
though child you are
and often you laugh.

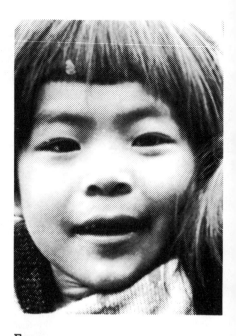

For you are
of the ancient race –
tens of thousands of years
of unwritten history,
sleeping quietly
in the depth
of your dark eyes,
revealing everything –
yet nothing –
of the nameless sorrow
of something forever lost.

Something about you
enchants
and enraptures.
You are so young.
No one has spoiled you
or marred
or stained you
yet
with sin.

And your beauty
is the haunting cry,
the dreadful tragedy
of all true beauty –
always destroyed
by greed
and lust.

For we wish to possess
what can only be gazed at.
We wish to own
what can only be sung –
by the light
in our eyes
and the beat
of our heart.

And thus
I remember you –
evanescent brightness
on the canvas
of human tragedy –
and rejoice
in your beauty,
which you wear
in grace
and the dignity
of innocence
that God gave you.
And you delight him
with his own creation.

Waswanipi (Light on Water)

To Alcatraz the Indians went.
We questioned their defiance,
and wondered what these people meant
in sudden self-reliance.
And then we heard of Wounded Knee –
but no one knows Waswanipi.

It all began in Miquelon
where shacks smelled of cheap liquor.
The trapping's finished, game is gone
(the welfare cheques are quicker),
and beer drowns out your misery –
for no one knows Waswanipi.

The fisheries some profit showed
(and hard they worked and well).
At Quevillon the pulpmill flowed –
poisoned the River Bell.
The fish filled up with mercury –
for no one knows Waswanipi.

The mines came to Matagami.
The Indians moved around.
There was no room there for the Cree –
they don't go underground.
The copper price is strong, you see –
and no one knows Waswanipi.

Then roads were stretched and bridges flung –
Baie James! Hydro Quebec!
And fancy white man's homes were strung
around the red man's shack.
We can't stop progress, you'll agree –
and no one knows Waswanipi.

The trucks roar on – an endless line –
across the River Bell.
Between the Hydro and the mine
there's only the hotel.
Soon lakes will rise and none will see
or weep – for lost Waswanipi.

When the roads were built, the Waswanipi
band scattered to find work in various
places along the roads, and the Hudson's
Bay Company closed its post on the lake.
The Waswanipi were the first inland Cree
people to feel the full impact of twentieth
century society.

The Graves

The Chief
did not answer you
directly
Maitre.
He had too much civilization
to do that –
to lash back
with the same viciousness
that you displayed.

It's easy
Maitre,
with your education
your background,
to attempt
to show up an Indian
who must use an interpreter.
You are not only
a language apart,
but more –
a thousand tears
a choked cry
a silence
of sorrow.

You
did not have to dig
your mother's grave
yourself
Maitre,
in the dead of winter
in the awesome silence
of the bush –
did you?

You did not sit up
all that night
when Elizabeth
became so ill,
and worry
all that night
and the next day
and into the long night
again,
when all of a sudden
her flushed face
became very white
and very still
and very cold.

It was not
your tears
that fell
on Elizabeth's face
that day
when the cry of distress
seemed frozen
in the still air.

It was not you
Maitre,
who once again
went to dig a grave,
reading portions
from the battered
prayer book.

It was not you
Maitre,
whose voice was heard
that day,
breaking
when the hymn was sung
and the prayer said.

When your mother
was buried
Maitre,
there was grief
certainly,
measured sorrow
restrained by ceremony
and those who know
what to do.
There was also
the parish priest
to soothe it,
with the dispassionate
majesty of the Requiem.

There was the funeral director
with his cool
correct efficiency
and just the right touch
of everything,
and all of that
was very comforting.
And the labourers came
afterwards
to fill in the grave,
when you had already gone
in the black limousine.

The chief said, 'There will be a great effect on
my people. But there is something else. My
people have relatives buried on their trap-
lines along the Eastmain River. Even myself.
I have five children who are buried along the
river and on my trapline. My mother is
buried there also. These bodies of our relatives are very sacred to us and we do not
want to see them buried under water.' The
lawyer asked the chief if he thought the
buried dead would be any worse off. The
chief replied, 'The reason why I'm saying
this is because I'm against the project, and
my people are also.'

Have you ever
carried a dead child
Maitre,
the cold
limp body
in your arms?
Have you ever
dug a grave
with your own hands?
Have you ever
knelt in prayer
in the cold snow,
under a powerless sun
in the few hours' daylight
in the silence
of the north,
your tears frozen
where they mark
the ground?

The ground is sacred
because of those tears,
those bodies lying there
awaiting the resurrection
at the Last Day.

But you
would not understand
Maitre,
you think only of progress
and snowmobiles
and outboards
bringing benefits to those
who do not even
speak your language,
whose children
you have never seen,
whose eyes
have never enchanted you,
whom you have never kissed
or carried or played with
or prayed for or buried.

You talk
of progress
and development
to these people
who will never understand.

I pray
that you will never
have to bury your children
Maitre,
or have your mother's grave
flooded by progress.
I do not wish it on you.
I only wish
you would
understand.

Lilly

Play
little Lilly,
with the slingshot
your grandfather made –
because he has leisure here,
and he is sober
in the bush.

Play
little Lilly.
Run about
on the small snowshoes
your grandmother made
from the last moose –
for she, too, has time
in the bush.

Play
little Lilly.
Look!
Your mother is laughing.
Here, she has time
to play with you –
with none of that white trash
hanging around,
one of whom is your father.
But he doesn't know.
He has never seen
the loveliness of your eyes.

Soon
too soon
far too soon,
someone will buy
your body
with a bottle of beer,
and your submission
with a welfare cheque.

Play
little Lilly,
play in innocence
play in your untamed loveliness.
None of it will last very long,
and there is only
a lifetime
of agony
to come,
of unending
alcoholic nightmares
and being pushed around
and abused.

The land you live on
will be flooded
by water,
as your life
will be flooded
by tears.

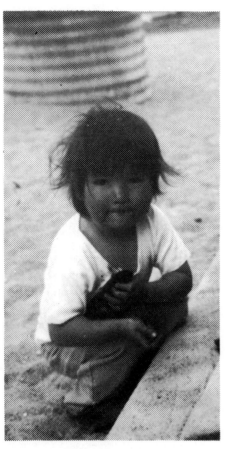

As I sit on this log
watching you
I offer you candy
chocolate,
hoping for a smile
waiting anxiously
for you to come to me –
just for a moment.
I am buying
the light of your eyes
with a candy.

Apology

For a moment –
ten incredible days
intoxicating in unbelief –
it had happened.
(Indians do win in court.)
The judge had ordered
to cease and desist
the James Bay project.

An iron curtain fell
over that country –
not even the press got in
and no one was saying much.
We wondered and then waited
for the trucks to move out.

The appeals court
was very swift and decisive,
lifting the injunction
on grounds of the greater good –
because the good of some people
outweighs the good of other people
Because the good of the white man
outweighs the good of the Cree.

The curtain was lifted
and darkness fell.
It was the same day
in November
when the United States
remembered the murder
of a president,
but no one here
remembers the assassination
of a people.

There was a baby to be baptized
(as always in an Indian settlement),
and I went, as always.
But this time
it was not a pleasant trip –
the trailers and trucks
were moving north once more.
I passed many
but I could not hold them back.

The moment
when you hold the little child,
look down on the small face
the black hair
and those dark eyes,
can be a time
of great happiness –
but not always.

I want to apologize, Jacob,
on behalf of my country
the province I live in
the church I serve
the race I belong to,
and for myself as well.

I am glad I brought you
into the family of God
and laid you in his arms.
There alone you will find
you are accepted.
There alone you will be
a human being
of infinite value –
but there alone.

I must apologize, Jacob,
because in this country
there are two kinds of people,
and the good of some
always exceeds
the good of others,
and I belong to the one kind
but you to the other.
We all have the same rights –
paper rights for you
that sound beautifully
and read truly
but can be overruled
by the other kind of people
who have the real rights.

So here you are.
Is there a terrible significance
in the fact I am already
looking down on you?
You are a bundle of life
in my arms, Jacob,
yet you are a non-person
a non-citizen
with no rights.

I am sorry
ashamed to share in this.
I may protest it
yet it is part of me
because I belong
to the other kind of people,
the ones with all the rights –
the rights that weigh heavily.

Never before
have my arms felt so heavy,
carrying not a baby
but the burden of sin.
Away from me, Lord,
for I am a sinful man.

These arms God uses
to hold you, Jacob,
are unclean –
for they also
reach for power.
They may cuddle you
my little brother,
but do not ever trust them.
They can choke
and squeeze
and strangle
to possess.

God, I ask you
to take care of Jacob,
for we will not.
We'll make objections
reasoned well and cogently
as soon as care costs money
and we have to give
of what we have –
and worse,
of what we are –
as soon as we must admit
that Jacob is as precious
and important
to you
as the blue-eyed child
of the engineer
or the grandchild
of the appeal court's judge.

Here, Margaret
mother of sorrows,
take him
hold him
before I soil him.
And may God bless you
Jacob,
and have mercy
on us all,
for all our righteousness
is as filthy rags.

There is no soundness in us
no health,
only the disease of power
that chokes
and strangles
and kills.
We have done it
to the least of his brethren.
We have done it
to him.
We have sinned
against heaven
and before thee,
and are no more worthy
to be called thy sons.

Winnie

Why did I stop there?
I was in a hurry
and certainly had enough to do,
and they always
have something to ask you.
Perhaps I just wanted to sit
in the few tents by the roadside
with people that weren't in a hurry,
that were not always thinking
of the things they had to do.

Winnie asked,
'Will you find out
what they have done
with my baby?'
Yes, Winnie, I will.
Is it Matthew you mean,
when the nurse came
and said he was sick
and took him with her?
Sure, I'll find out.

That's what you get for stopping –
more work, more things to do.
Drive faster. You must get back
before the offices close,
and all these long distance calls
are expensive.
But Winnie is worried.

At the Health Services
they are somewhat impatient.
'Yes, of course
we told her everything.
Why don't these people understand?
We tell them, and explain
two, three, ten times even,
and then they act
as if they don't know
anything of what we said.
Why don't they realize
we do the best for their children?'

I think I could tell you,
snappy, efficient
little office nurse
sitting behind your desk
already tidy,
watching the clock
that says ten to five,
I can picture the whole thing
just from the tone of your voice.
I think I know why these people
never understand
but I won't say it –
you would not understand.

Just tell me all you know
about the baby's health.
Bandnumber one-five-three
yes, that's right.
His name is Matthew.
I know it says
Lawrence Matthew on the list
but he is known by his last name.
And I have to call back tomorrow
because it's closing time now
and you can't get the file?

You don't understand
that Winnie is worried
as any mother would be –
your mother, too.
Winnie can't talk in French.
She doesn't care about numbers,
band numbers
telephone numbers
or whether it's five to five now.
She wants to know only
if Matthew is all right.

What hospital then?
You can't tell me?
What nonsense is that?
Oh, the other nurse was in charge
and she arranged the admission
and she wont be back
till next week?
Why don't I phone Indian Affaires?
Yes, why don't I?
Because it's another phone call,
the twelfth or the thirteenth
in three days,
and I'll only speak to someone
who doesn't know
or doesn't care
and who refers me back to you,
or is out of town
or not in the office today.

And it's fifty miles
where Winnie lives
and I have my work to do
also.

But Winnie is worried
and I try again.
And after the second call
I get a nurse at the hospital
who knows something
and she, bless her heart,
calls sister supervisor.
And the nun is a woman
who understands and cares
about sick children
and worried mothers,
and she gives me all
Winnie wants to know.
Que Dieu vous bénisse, soeur –
God bless you.

Fifty miles
isn't really all that long
when you have good news.
The way back is easy.

A worried face
breaking into a smile,
relief doing wonderful things
to her expression –
dark eyes
kindling with light.
And Winnie says,
'I knew you would come.'
She knew I would.
I did not think I'd drive
that road again today.
Perhaps she does understand.

Possessing

A few geese
winged their way north,
flying low,
weary
in the grey silence
of early morning –
for winter still lingered
and dawn was cold.

Then from the east
the first rays of sunlight
struck them,
before sweeping
the land below.
Their breast feathers
flashed white.
Their wings beat dark
against the sky.
And their wild voices
rejoiced.

My heart soared
to see such beauty –
I had no need for food
no desire to kill for sport,
to tense up and worry them
within range of the gun,
to feel excitement
as the moment comes near
for them to die.

My heart was at peace
yet thrilled by this sight.
For suddenly I knew –
to enjoy such beauty
I must lose all desire
to possess it.

For to own
these wild creatures
I must kill
they must die –
lose their life and beauty.
But then
I would die a little
also.

Is not all possessing
a way of destroying?
Was this not the secret
discovered by Saint Francis?
He enjoyed all things
and refused to own any.
All things were his –
he would not possess them
master
destroy them,
bring them into subjection.
He left them
in God's hands.

Seeing these geese
I realized my freedom,
freedom from desire
to possess.
They were mine
because I did not own them.
I was free to live
because they lived –
they winging their way
northward,
I with my prayer
of thanksgiving
winging happily to God,
who made us one
in the freedom
of his love.

James Bay Settlement

Someone
called it a victory,
a paper victory
perhaps –
paper money
paper agreements
paper cheques.
For you have to do things
our way now
with all kinds of paper –
documents, studies, briefs
contracts, agreements
and televised signing ceremonies
with everyone smiling
paper smiles.

That's why we need your forests –
so we can turn them into paper.
That's what all these trees are for,
aren't they? –
newspapers and legal submissions
art magazines and comics
record jackets and pornography
academic dissertations
and grocery bags.

Land
in exchange
for paper,
promises signed
on dead trees,
hopes traded
for dollar bills.

Already
the trucks wind their way
down the wandering lumber roads.
They're always the first –
swaying
under their loads of pulpwood
to be turned into more paper
more dollar bills
more promises.

Land turned to paper
land put on paper –
dead land.
Even the paper I write on
is dead, too.
No words will make it live
like the trees
singing in the forests.

That land –
vast, immense
as its overpowering silences,
majestic as the rivers
sweeping down –
its lakes shimmering
under the whispers
of the Northern Lights,
exuberant as the cry
of the wild geese
in the high skies.

That land
cannot be put on paper
nor expressed in promises.
It can only be shared with God
and the people he placed there.

Now that land will wither,
grow old, yellow
brittle.
It will break and tear,
and little shreds
will disappear
somewhere on the way
to nothing.

We all have our price
our paper price –
political gain
or paper cheques,
a well paying job
with a fancy title –
co-ordinator
chief consultant –
a new house, a skidoo
a case of beer
a book of paper poems.
But all the words
written on that paper
are only signs
of lamentation
and mourning
and woe.

We may have conquered
James Bay
(as the Premier
said we would),
and you may have won
your victory
(as the magazine article
said you did),
but we have **not** conquered
ourselves.

And you did not win –
no one won.
We simply
all lost.

Metamorphosis

The Northern Lights were leaping
in free and fickle flight.
Below, the truck lights creeping
tore up the silent night.

the Lights were softly rustling
in sweet, soft hushing sound,
but trucks with engines hustling,
their swishing silence drowned.

Where once wild geese were winging –
their trumpet calls had flared –
now office phones were ringing
and television blared.

Where once the loon laughed lonely,
and moose their bellows rang,
the game had left – and only
drunk tourists laughed and sang.

For white men hate the silence –
they shatter it with sound
and strike it down with violence,
till all the quiet's drowned.

No longer raced the river,
for stubborn dams stood still.
Its flow had stopped forever –
the lakes began to fill.

The waters still were rising.
Dead trees stood bare, forlorn.
Mist veiled the far horizon –
no evening, and no morn.

The Northern Lights still glimmer,
but city lights, too bright,
reduce them till they shimmer –
then dies their gentle light.

Culture

They sat in their shack,
old Solomon and Maria,
Charlie their youngest son,
and Sophie.
I just married them
last summer.

Charlie and Sophie
both went to school.
They learned to read English,
the ways of Western civilization.

They were reading
when I came in.
I saw the magazine
between them
on the rickety wooden table
in their corner of the room.
It looked strangely
out of place –
the flashy cover
among left-over beaver
and a plate
of half eaten fish.
It was a magazine
with nude girls
and articles about sex.
Charlie and Sophie
looked so solemn,
as if they were studying
a serious book
or even the Bible.

They closed the magazine
when I came in
but they were not embarrassed.
Charlie just went to get me a chair
and Sophie to see about some coffee.
It was I who was embarrassed.
It made me wonder,
Is this what we hand on
of our civilization
to those who enter it today?

Is this all
they will ever know
of the world
that painted a Sistine Chapel
and built Chartres
and Cologne,
that called forth a Shakespeare
and sings the melodies of Mozart?

We come with pornography
as we came with small pox
and TB
and always, of course,
with alcohol
and lately
with mercury.

Sure
we wiped out the smallpox,
and we control TB
very well today,
but now we have
something new to offer –
Minimata disease.
Even the name
sounds appropriately Indian –
for it only strikes Indians.
Why do they eat so much fish?
Why can't they eat cake
and fish for fun –
and go hungry for fun.
And the Japanese got it too –
so you're not the only ones.
And Japanese lives were cheap
in Nagasaki,
and Indian lives are cheap
around Kenora.

We talk of acculturation,
which somehow or other
ends up as pornography
on your table, Charlie,
with the left-over beaver.
And one of these days
you might make enough money
to get yourself a television set.
Then you can hear our politicians
condemning racism in Rhodesia.

Acculturation in our hands
brings the filth
and not the civilization
the worst
and never the best
the ugly
and not the beautiful
the noise
and never the harmony.

I don't know the answer
Charlie,
or Sophie
with that clean
and lovely smile,
so strikingly different
from the smile
of the girl
on the cover.

I am deeply ashamed,
as if I had written
and produced that magazine,
to give to you
and to Sophie
to pervert your soul
and soil
her clean
and lovely smile.

The Yellow Shirt

Young Charlie Matoosh
went to work for the Mines,
far away from his home,
Mistassini –
three months to make money,
a contract for lines,
and in summer
he'd marry his Minnie.

There were four of them there
on the line-cutting crew,
and the chores
they would all share together.
Their lines through bush
ran quickly and true
as they laboured
in sub-zero weather.

Each week the Beaver
would fly in supplies –
there were always letters
for Charlie –
and once Abel ordered
a little surprise –
four cases of beer
for a party.

In the mail was a parcel
that Minnie had sent –
a beautiful dress-shirt,
bright yellow.
He put it on quickly
as they sat in the tent,
and the beer made their mood
warm and mellow.

Charlie felt hot,
took a breather outside –
he was lonesome for Minnie
and thinking.
Then he saw the skidoo,
and he felt like a ride –
the others were busy
with drinking.

The skidoo took off fast.
Charlie laughed in his joy,
and left,
all his sadness forgotten.
With the white man's beer
and the white man's toy,
he raced off –
in the shirt of thin cotton.

Four miles out he got stuck,
and he tried hard to push –
as they saw by his tracks
all around him.
But the cold was too much
for Charlie Matoosh,
and only that morning
they found him.

The police flew in.
Their conclusion was short –
how Charlie had frozen
and perished.
No mention was made
in their brief report
that he wore the new shirt
he had cherished.

The mining bosses
were decent enough –
to the nearest town
had him hurried.
They sent Minnie his cheque
along with his stuff
save the shirt –
in which he was buried.

They gave a nice stone
and took pictures to send –
so that Minnie could see
and remember.
It would take many months
for her sorrow to mend,
and the baby was due
in November.

The Meeting

She was thirteen –
standing strangely defiant
by the road.
She was hitch-hiking.
I knew right away
something was wrong,
for Cree people aren't defiant.
I stopped.
She recognized me –
too late.
There was no escape.

'Come, Alice,
I'll take you home.'
But she would not.
She was thirteen
and scared
and angry –
and very drunk.

We talked.
I talked –
she listened
not at all.
For a long time
it was like that.
Then she let loose –
anger flashing suddenly
and boldly,
scared as she was –
stabbing me with words.

Yes, she was going
to hitch-hike.
She was going
to kill herself.
She was never going back
to that goddamn school
or to my goddamn church
anymore.

And on she went –
the dam broke
and the waters
of bitterness
swept over me,
drowning me
in their violence.
Ever faster
she continued,
finding all the swear words
all the filthy obscenities –
the worst garbage
picked up
from my white-man's language,
flung at me
in her fury.
And I stood still,
shocked
and shamed.

There was something
magnificent
about her –
that scared
little
thirteen-year old,
drunk
and defiant,
calling me down.
For I was white,
and represented the world
the school, the church
authority –
all that was closing in
on her
relentlessly –
everything she resented.

It was strangely beautiful
the way she stood –
pouring out in wild
cruel words,
the agony
of a misunderstood people –
years of sorrow
and suppressed anger.
Blackflies clouded around.
Cars whistled by,
the dust settling on me
like the grey hopelessness
of her words.

Until it was all gone,
and she sat down
and cried
and talked quietly –
but still desperately –
and listened finally
to my feeble words
of white man's comfort.
There was too much
I could not say.

So I took care of her
and brought her
to the hospital,
because she had simply
broken down,
and there was really
nowhere else to go.

And a gentle nun
dressed in white
took her to a room.
And they gave her
a clean white bed,
the white man's way –
with white sheets.
And a nurse all in white
gave her some white pills.
But her black hair
could not be tamed
and flowed victoriously
over the pillow.

And I sat with her
a long time.
Her hands still trembled –
so I held them,
and found that way
I could say things
that words could not,
and I said very little.
The silence grew
and we understood.

And she was very beautiful
when she fell asleep,
the tear marks
still on her face –
but peace was there also.

She went home
a few days after,
and never
talked to me again.
She had said too much,
revealed something
that had to be hidden
from me,
the white man
the priest
the eternal stranger.

And even though
I did not mention anything
of what had passed,
she never said another word.
And her silence hurt me
more than all
those bitter words.
In the end
it was her silence –
how she would look away –
that killed something
in me.

Andrew

A friend said,
'Write something happier,
not always of tragedy and death.
Surely there is happiness also.'

At once I thought of Andrew.
He stood tall
and walked with grace.
Never did I see a man
with such incredible poise.
He was at home everywhere –
in church
where he would read
the lessons in soft,
easy flowing Cree
(sounds of rivers
under Northern Lights,
of wind in timeless forests).

He was at ease
in my living room
(though that was foreign to him),
or again
on the street
where I might meet him –
never in haste,
always self-assured
pleasant and smiling
in his casual dignity.
He knew who he was –
and it was good.

He was a magnificent man,
attractive in his quiet charm
that breathed peace,
a serene nobility.
I envied him.

He preferred to live in a tent,
and he had asked his father
to choose a wife for him
who had not gone to school.
For once girls went there
they were trouble,
always complaining,
and they forgot
how to make good food.
Andrew was right.
His wife had two sisters
who had gone to school
and there was trouble all the time –
marriage, money, children.
All was cursed.

He was often right.
He knew.
He had three years of school –
enough to speak English
French and Cree,
enough to get a job
enough to understand
and read and write a bit –
all he wanted
from the white mans' language.

He was a superb hunter,
the guide always in demand,
for he was a good companion
with his charm and good looks
and easy laughter.
The mining bosses wanted him
for surveys, staking, exploration.
He worked well and fast
and didn't go off drinking.
And Andrew would say, 'Yes,'
or often, 'No, not now'.
He only worked for wages
when he needed money.
He was free.

He'd work a few months,
do the job, and do it well.
Then he was free again
to hunt a little
to go to the lake and live there,
catching fish and being himself
with his wife and children.

He didn't need much money.
He didn't want a house –
'It closes in on you,' he said.
He liked the small tent
in the vast country.

He was no one's slave
and no one's master.
He knew what freedom was
and walked in it with grace.

That is the happy story.

Yet his life also came apart.
His wife fell in
with a zealous sect
and got so religious
he found life difficult.
It was hard to be at home.
She was trying all the time
to get him out of one church
into the other.
He could not walk outside
for it was winter.
He went to the hotel.
It took his freedom –
not when he staggered out
but when he went in.

And all of a sudden
one of his children died,
and three others ended up
in the sanatorium.
I met him there once
when he was visiting them.
The light had left his eyes.
His steps were slow
and heavy
on the stone stairs.

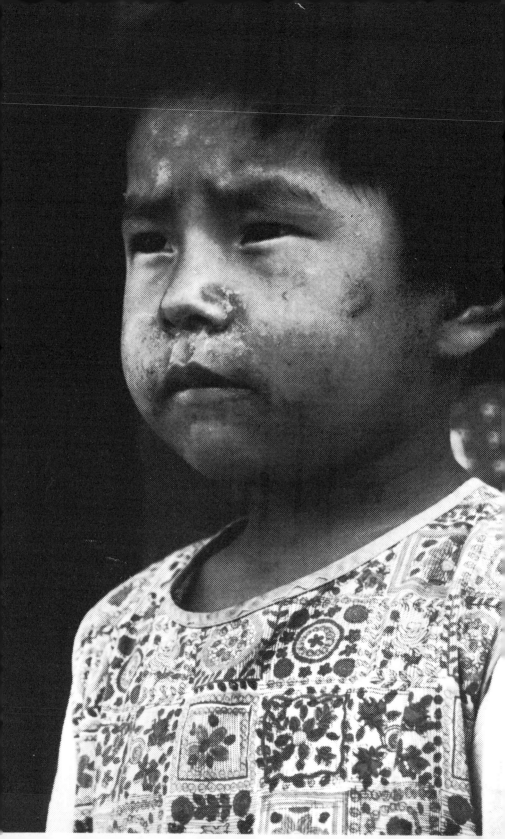

Andante Favori

Judy, with your smile delighting
though your eyes are always sad,
with spontaneous joy exciting –
to behold you makes me glad.

Playful as an otter are you,
carefree as the geese in flight.
Nothing seems to hurt or scar you.
All seems lovely, happy, bright.

Your smile is happy.
Your eyes are sad.
Your father is drunk,
and your mother is dead.

Always there are friends and others
to extend their help and care.
In your race all men are brothers –
no unwanted children there.

Laughing, people would behold you,
and Tohan they named you, 'Ball.'
None would ever think to scold you
with your smile delighting all.

Your smile is happy.
Your eyes are sad.
Your father is drunk,
and your mother is dead.

How I wish that I could take you,
for my home's a 'better place.'
Yet what right have I to break you
from your own and ancient race?

Play along, and jump in laughter.
Bounce Tohan in gladness, free.
Sorrow surely will come after –
such is fated for the Cree.

Judy, with your smile enchanting
though your eyes are always sad,
silent shadows stalk there haunting–
father drunk, and mother dead.

A Meaningful Role

They are our people,
we all agreed.
And the church must act
to be the church in the world.
And we have to ensure
that Native peoples.
can also celebrate life –
which we know
means something different
from celebrating in a tavern
or buying a case of beer
with the welfare cheque.

Very well. We agree.
We will call a meeting
and set up a committee
with an executive
which appoints a task force
for an in-depth study
requiring resource persons –
not the ones who live there
for these are too involved.
We need academics
from universities around us,
people who have a reputation
a well known name.
They can be counted upon
to put it all in the right way
and the ongoing terms.

The task force brings in
the report
with its striking title
and fancy printing,
and the executive reconvenes
the committee
which moves resolutions
to be sent to Synod
and which are debated
very thoroughly
on the floor of Synod,
and amendments are moved
and discussed in turn,
and one or two motions
are tabled
for they are rather controversial,
but at least we have agreed
to establish a permanent committee
to explore meaningful avenues
to relate relevantly to the issues
of our time
and our role
and our need to be
the church in the world.
We have really done
much work
and have met at length,
and we are
very concerned.

Certainly, it takes time
to organize, appoint,
vote, elect.
Years pass.
We take this very seriously,
and synods don't meet
every year.

Waters are rising
near James Bay.
Every now and then
there are disturbing reports
claiming very few Native people
are employed there.
And there is drilling
in the Beaufort Sea.
And the pipeline preparations
are proceeding very well
as the cost of energy rises
impressing all of us
with the need for fuel.
It may be Alberta's oil
but certainly not the Inuit's land,
and the moose have gone
and the caribou diminished
and the fish are poisoned
and the Indians stirred up
and the Eskimo angry
and the Metis hostile.

It is time to call
another meeting
and create a council
of concern.
But let us make very certain
only the right people
are concerned
the right way –
not the ones who might offend
a minister of the Crown
or who would say intemperate words
about the French in Quebec.
And let us by all means
study the problem
from every side,
in depth.

In the next generation –
when our children
will be asked what we did
and where the church was
when the land was flooded
and people dying of mercury,
when teenagers committed suicide
and the jail population
was proportionally so much higher
for Native people
(Yes, that also needs
some fact finding.
Could we hire
an eminent criminologist
or perhaps
a lay delegate to Synod
with a degree in sociology
to investigate the situation?)

Our children will be able
to show the Native peoples
the records
of successive Synods,
when the matter was all
discussed at length
and explored in depth
and researched at the grass roots.
They can point to all
the books we wrote
the reports we printed
the articles we published,
the submissions made
the resolutions resolved
the people appointed
the committees called.

As you can see
we are very concerned.
It's all on the record.

Bella And Lizzie

The scandal sheets screamed it,
slavering heavy-worded
over hideous details
real or imagined –
though reality was worse
than their sick revelling.

The more responsible papers
had some ten lines
on an inside page.
'The bodies of two young
Indian girls
fifteen and sixteen,
bound together with rope
were discovered in a gravel pit
near Highway 113
north of Senneterre.
Police identified the girls
as Bella and Lizzie
of Mistassini Indian Reserve.'

Even now
I can't tell the story
of Bella and Lizzie,
who were hitchhiking
when three men picked them up.

Some ten days later
I had to travel that road.
The forest was still hushed –
it was late October.

Winter had not yet come
that year,
but the trees
were bare already
waiting for the cold.
No wind.
Nothing moved that day.
'I looked on the earth
and lo, it was waste and void,
and to the heavens
but they had no life.
There was no man,
and all the birds of the air
had fled.'*

Somewhere along here –
this desolate stretch
of gravel road
that I knew so well
and now know
in another way.
One could feel it
in the awesome silence,
but the trees did not tell
what they had seen,
and no echoes sounded.

Yet once again
the voice of blood shed
was crying to God
from the ground,
and I heard it
in the eery silence.
It was loud
and full of anguish.

*JER 4:23

69

In the court
the lawyers pleaded
for a change of venue.
Yet even the reporters
of the sick papers
gathering like fat
shiny flies
on summer garbage,
ready to feast
upon yet more details
of the refuse of humanity –
even they wondered
why the police had been afraid
(stationing extra guards that day),
even they marvelled
how civilized and quiet
the Indians were.
As if the savages would seek
bloody revenge
for their murdered
savagely mutilated children.
Now that would have been
something to write about.

No, I cannot write
of Bella and Lizzie
foolish as they were,
hitchhiking
looking for excitement.
Don't you know
what that means?
Don't you know
not to get into cars
with white men?

But I now know
what it means
in the book of Genesis
when God says to Cain
he's heard his brother's blood
crying from the ground.

I heard it also
that day,
which was waste and void
in the timeless silence
of that eery forest.

It was loud
and full
of anguish.

The Geese And The Vultures

Longer than memory
the geese have returned
in spring –
not the overwhelming flocks
of October,
but small groups
searching for open water –
their cries exuberant,
making your heart
jump with joy.

Now change has come
and men sweep in –
not like the geese.
Their cries are frightening,
making your heart
sink in cold fear.

They fly in with planes
and helicopters –
vultures in hardhats
and business suits.
What is this madness,
this frantic rush
to get their hands
on everything –
wood, water,
minerals, rocks,
even living things –
a quest for security
a desire for power?

Soon airstrips appear
calling for bigger planes
bringing ever more engineers
to doctor the country,
each with his own
scientific way
of violating nature.
Then the machines
the tractors
the inevitable bulldozers
roaring like maddened beasts –
steel fangs cutting
biting
leveling the land
into a hopeless
deformity.

What is this dream
of progress
and development
that always turns
into screeching nightmares –
the clanking of a thousand gears
the roar of a thousand engines
from which there is no awakening?

What do they have to prove –
that they can produce
more pulp and paper
more copper
gold, zinc
megawatts
than anyone else
in the world –
and consume it, too?
Why do they have to boast
of having the biggest dam
the largest man-made lake
the longest road
the strongest bridge?
Can they not boast
of serenity
of harmony
and peace?

Once the engineers
have done their work –
the construction finished
the high paying jobs over –
then come the tourists.
They are not bad people –
many of them quiet
decent folk,
just wanting to camp
here,
to try for some trout
there,
and do some hunting
(geese or ducks
just a few,
only one moose),
all according
to the game laws,
everything legal
licensed.

Each will take
just his quota,
but it will be multiplied
a thousand fold,
leaving less
for those who still depend
on what the land provides –
food that makes the difference
between comfort
and near starvation
in the long winter,
when often you must live
off the impoverished land.

The tourists
will take their pictures
for the folks back home,
of quaint
and curious Indians
in shacks and tents.
How dirty
how terrible
these living conditions!
Can't something be done
for them?

It has been done
already –
not **for** them
but **to** them.
Come,
take your pictures
quickly
before they vanish
forever –
into your slums
and skidrows
and jails.

The geese leave in the fall
with a promise to return.
But the vultures stay on
winging vicious circles
searching always
watching for more
more and more
to own and use
to possess
and to consume.

Go away, Indian,
disappear.
No one wants you.
You do not fit our computers
our programmes
and our progress.
We did not know
you were still living here.
But now that we know
we do not care.

We've taken the pictures
shot the home movies.
Your children's smiles
will be on our slides
in cozy living rooms
across the continent.
Now, go away,
die.
You bother us
just being here.
You say something –
even in your silence –
that we don't want
to hear.

Where Are You

Where are you
Rosanne?
with your French name
given you by a French nurse –
most appropriate,
for your father is French
though no one knows him.
Not even your mother
is sure.

She brought you
to church
anyway –
to be baptized.
Few people were there
that cold December Sunday,
and no one wanted to stand .
as godparent
for an illegitimate
halfbreed kid,
conceived
in some drunken binge.

So I stood
and I baptized you,
held you in my arms –
precious little bundle
of debris,
thrown on the shore
of humanity.

Soon after that
you were adopted
and disappeared
from my life.
Your mother didn't care.
She was always running around
with anyone she could find –
and there sure were plenty
to take advantage
of that!

But once more we met –
in hospital –
and I thought I knew you
and checked out your name.
You were almost a year old –
a hauntingly beautiful
little girl,
clean and lovely
in spite of the senseless lust
that brought you life –
black eyes boring
into the depth
of my uneasy soul.

I know now
I should have adopted you,
for every night
when I lift you up
before the throne of God,
I wonder
where you are –
those eyes still burning
into my soul,
asking the question
I did not have courage
to answer.

I wonder
where you are –
with some good French family,
soon going to school?
Will your Indian blood
reveal itself
inspite of all
the white surroundings?
Will they laugh at you
in school
when they see
that you are different?

Where are you
Rosanne?
I cannot shake those haunting
burning eyes,
in which there smoulders
the agony
of a doomed people.

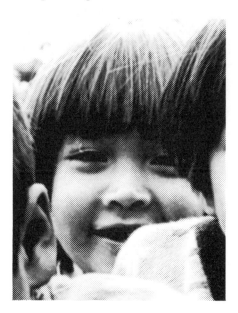

Janet.

She stood by the highway
diffident in the summer wind
looking no more than fifteen
thumb raised half-heartedly.

She did not even realize
I had stopped.
She expected me to drive past
and almost I did.
Then I remembered
Bella and Lizzie.
I had to make up for that.

She was nineteen,
a slight shadow of a girl.
She told me she was going back
to see her father for a while,
after many years.

In spite of all
my white man's questions,
which she answered
with that resigned patience
which experience in our world
had brought her,
I could not make much sense
out of the story.
It was puzzling,
a series
of disconnected statements.
She stayed somewhere
near Orillia.
She was going somewhere
beyond Kenora.
A typical Indian story –
Indian stories always
lack a why.

No money.
No luggage.
Just a jacket
only slightly frayed.
Indians never seem to need
things to carry around.
They just wander –
free.

She was so vulnerable.
I had to think again
of Bella and Lizzie
who stood by a road once also,
and were found
a few days later –
dead.
I shivered
thinking,
How long before it's you?
That's why I stopped –
to delay that moment,
to prove not all of us
are savages,
and for a few hundred miles
she would be safe.

She leaned back her head
as soon as I had finished
the inevitable questions.
Haven't you learned yet
not to trust anyone?
Haven't you read
about Bella and Lizzie
and all the others?
Am I the one who has to tell you?
But she was asleep already,
that sweet vulnerability
tangible
asking for a response –
care and protection
or the opposite –
giving you the choice
to be a savage
or a saint.

Am I doing you a favour,
building up a trust
that might be ripped apart
perhaps the next ride?
Yet, what can I do?
She'll go her way
no matter what I say.
I am as helpless
as you are, Janet.

I detoured a bit –
just thirty miles extra for me
but fifty nearer for her –
fifty miles more
before that moment
that I feared
and she did not.

Have you eaten lunch?
Nothing since that coffee
that was your breakfast?
Of course. I knew that.
Hungry?
'Yes.'
I bought her a meal.
She looked puzzled.
Why would I do that,
but she did not ask why.
They never do.
She ate hungrily
and did what I said –
put those buns in her pocket
to keep going somewhere
along the way
sometime.

And when finally
I had to turn off,
I slipped her some money –
buying the honour of my race
with a few dollars
from the discretionary fund.

She got out
as she had come in –
with that shy smile.
I looked in the mirror
as I started up again.
I went on my way
and she on hers.
How different these ways!

She looked and waved,
happy in her vulnerable
freedom.
I wonder how she managed?
Perhaps God kept her on her way.
All the way back
I prayed for that.

Twelve Impromptus
Of A Scattered People

The little lake close by Joutel
is marked 'Terrain Privé,'
and guards stand by the River Bell.
'You can't pass here,' they say.
'No one allowed. None enters here
except men for Baie James.'
Now even we are strangers here,
and none will hear our claims.
We cannot understand this greed.
To us it makes no sense.
the land was here, and none had need
of signs or guards or fence.

At Doré Lake we used to stay
till copper there was found.
The mine boss said to move away.
'We don't want you around.'
Their homes were built on land we own
where buried lay our dead.
We asked them, leave these graves alone.
'Come, move those bones,' they said.

Game wardens came and seized our meat.
Right in our camps they'd go.
We asked them what we now should eat.
They said they did not know.
Where Philip had his trapline set
this club came with skidoos.
In summer they would rip his net.
In fall they'd shoot his moose.
He says he can't find any game –
the beaver all are gone.
His line was on a mining claim –
so nothing could be done.

The anthropologists arrive
when spring comes to the land.
They pry into our ways and lives
with notebooks in their hand.
And for a study on the Cree
some even give us beer,
to make us talk for their degree.
And then they disappear.
The tourists come, more every year
now that the road is through.
With cameras they will soon appear
and act as in a zoo.
We'd rather they would not intrude,
But they don't seem to know
that in our way of life it's rude
to tell someone to go.

We'd teach our children on the land
to learn their father's way.
They put a school up for our band –
three hundred miles away.
The government officials came.
A school was all designed.
'Here's the paper. Put your name.
But none knew what he signed.
When kids come back,
there is a change.
Forgotten is their Cree.
They steal and cheat.
Their ways are strange
They're white men, now, we see.
Poor Jimmy, happy little fool
who always loved to roam.
He tried to run away from school
and hitch-hike his way home.
That night while we
were drinking beer,
the priest came in and said,
'I have bad news for you, I fear.
He's by the roadside, dead.'

Evadney went to Macamic,
'cause she had bad TB.
For seven years she lay there sick,
and none could speak in Cree.
When she returned, with laughter glad,
her eight-year old just stared.
She thought her mother was long dead
and she was really scared.

Isaiah went to the hotel.
A Frenchman robbed him there.
The policeman said, 'Oh, what the hell.
You Indians and your beer.'
They told him to go home, but he
got mad, began to fight.
You lose when you are drunk and Cree
and win when you are white.

The nurse who comes with good advice,
with bottles, pills, and care,
who gives the stuff to kill the lice
and checks the children's hair,
told us, 'This year eat no more fish.
It's poisoned through and through.
But cheques we'll give you as you wish.
We'll take good care of you.'
So now there's money to make sure
of poison we won't die.
And there's more cash to buy more beer –
in shacks the children cry.

Other churches with their books
came from the south to tell –
the church we went to was all wrong
and leading us to hell.
They pressured us our church to quit –
theirs was the truth alone.
Now, friends have parted, couples split,
and emnity has grown.
Some of the people got a scare,
and first they did quite well.
But now the saved in Senneterre
are back in the hotel.

Old Isaac drowned – good hunter he –
was born in a canoe.
He'd snowshoe from Waswanipi
but bought an old skidoo.
And he who knew the lake so well
lost feeling on that thing,
and through the ice old Isaac fell.
They found him in the spring.
And Ella, widowed, missed her man,
and she got very sick.
They sent her off. Now in the 'san'
she fades, in Macamic.

Old treaties say their words still stand
'as long as rivers flow,
long as the sun will warm the land
and grass in spring will grow.'
Perhaps that's why the dams are built –
to stop the rivers' run.
With fumes and dirt the grass is killed,
and smog now veils the sun.
Then we'll have larger lakes than these
but filled with mercury,
with poisoned fish and dying trees –
and vanish will the Cree.

The white man always asks the same,
and makes his paper fuss.
'Why don't you drop those Indian claims?
Why can't you be like us?'
'Why don't you get a job?' they say.
'Why don't you?' Why, why, why?
But in their hearts we hear them say,
'Why don't you people die.'